Bernacchi

Bernacchi

John Brown

One Man Against Slavery

by

Gwen Everett

paintings by

Jacob Lawrence

RIZZOLI
NEW YORK

We listened carefully to Father's reasons for wanting to end slavery.

None of us questioned his sincerity, for we knew he believed God created everyone equal, regardless of skin color. He taught us as his father had taught him: To own another person as property—like furniture or cattle—is a sin. When Father was twelve years old, he witnessed the cruel treatment of black men, women, and children held in bondage and he vowed, then and there, that one day he would put an end to the inhumanity.

"I once considered starting a school where free blacks could learn to read and write, since laws in the South forbid their education," he told us. "And, when we moved to North Elba, New York, we proved that black and white people could live together in peace and brotherhood."

"One person—one family—can make a difference," he said firmly. "Slavery won't end by itself. It is up to us to fight it."

Father called us by name: Mary, John, Jason, Owen, and Annie (me). He asked us to say a prayer and swear an oath that we, too, would work to end slavery forever. Then he told us his plan.

He would lead a small group of experienced fighting men into a state that allowed slavery. They would hide in the mountains and valleys during daylight. And, under the cover of night, members of this "liberation army" would sneak onto nearby plantations and help the slaves escape.

Freed slaves who wished to join Father's army would learn how to use rifles and pikes—spear-shaped weapons. Then, plantation by plantation, Father's liberation army would move deeper south—growing larger and stronger—eventually freeing all the slaves.

Father's idea sounded so simple. Yet my brothers and I knew this was a dangerous idea. It was illegal for black people to handle firearms and for whites to show them how. It was also against the law to steal someone else's property; and, in effect, Father was doing this by encouraging slaves to leave their masters.

That night I couldn't sleep. I wondered whether supplying people with weapons was the best way to end slavery. Why did my father feel the need to use deadly force? Why couldn't he write about slavery the way Harriet Beecher Stowe did in *Uncle Tom's Cabin*? Father gave me a copy of the book when I was eleven because it was one of his favorites. He told me that Mrs. Stowe became very popular among other abolitionists—people such as her and Father who wanted to end slavery. Her book helped change people's understanding of slavery.

I knew words could be powerful because each time I read the book I became angry that my own country had laws like the Fugitive Slave Law of 1850, which encouraged people to hunt down escaped slaves like animals.

Father could choose to use the pen to fight slavery, I decided.

Then I remembered the fighting in Kansas. Five of my older brothers were living there when the territory was applying for statehood. Fights between slavery supporters and abolitionists broke out over whether or not to allow slavery in the new state. One of the worst battles took place in May of 1856, when nearly 750 slavery supporters rode into Lawrence, Kansas, the headquarters for the abolitionists. The group terrorized the citizens and destroyed the town.

When he received my brothers' letter about the attack, Father left immediately to help.

Many called him a hero for fighting in Bloody Kansas, as it was known.

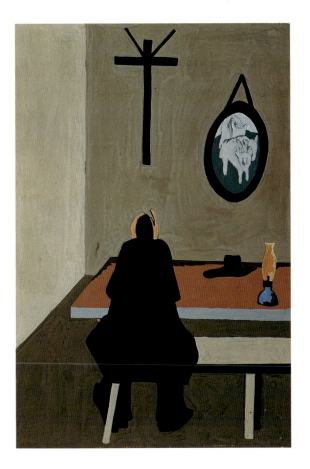

Others called him a killer. They said he murdered slavery supporters. I only know that when he returned, he was convinced that slavery would never end without more bloodshed. And he was determined to fight this evil practice, even if it meant losing his own life.

"I will die fighting for this cause. There will be no more peace in this land until slavery is done for," he declared.

I thought about his words as I tossed and turned in bed. Can one person really make a difference in correcting a national injustice? Is freedom worth dying for?

Another sleepless night I heard the sound of paper rustling in the kitchen. I tiptoed into the room and saw Father seated at the table, studying a map of the United States.

He thought aloud, "The Old Testament prophet Moses led people out of bondage. He talked to God on the mountaintop." He pointed to the South on the map. "And in the mountains that stretch from Virginia to Georgia, God will help me lead slaves to freedom."

Without looking up, he said: "Annie, just as one lamp can light an entire room, one person can touch the lives of many."

"Father, why don't you write a book about the black and white families who live here in North Elba?" I asked, knowing he was proud of our community.

North Elba came into being because Garritt Smith, one of New York's multimillionaires, donated one hundred thousand acres of land in the Adirondack Mountains to create a place where escaped slaves and whites could live and work together. Neighbors were always welcome in one another's homes and often shared meals together.

"Ending slavery is only the first battle," explained Father. "Most white abolitionists want to free the slaves, but some are not willing to actually live side by side with blacks as equals." He shook his head sadly and continued, "Some people believe that the only way to truly abolish slavery is to return all black people to Africa."

A few weeks later Father went to a convention of black abolitionists. It was held in a Canadian city in Ontario, called Chatham, where many escaped slaves from the United States lived. Among those attending were thirty-four black Canadians, several volunteers desiring to join Father's army, and one black abolitionist from Pittsburgh, Pennsylvania, Martin R. Delany.

At the convention Father revealed his plan to invade the South and use the mountains as natural forts. Then he presented a document he wrote called *The Provisional Constitution for the People of the United States.* It would form the basis of the laws to govern a new country where everyone was free and equal. Its preamble read:

"*. . .Therefore, we citizens of the United States, and the oppressed people, who, by a recent decision of the Supreme Court are declared to have no rights which the white man is bound to respect; together with all other people degraded by the laws thereof, do, for the time being ordain and establish for ourselves the following provisional constitution and ordinances, the better to protect our persons, property, lives, and liberties; and to Govern our Actions.*"

When I read Father's constitution, I realized the significance of his plan.

Father returned home with the support of many abolitionists in Canada and America. They promised to give him money and equipment.

"It is very expensive to equip and transport the men and supplies necessary to carry out my plan," he said. I then saw how valuable the help of his friends was when a group of six supporters gave large donations to his cause.

Father told us of an important meeting with the famous black abolitionist, speaker, and publisher, Frederick Douglass. He said Mr. Douglass was convinced that raiding the Harpers Ferry Armory and Arsenal in Virginia would hinder, not help, Father's mission. Mr. Douglass believed that the town was a "steel trap" from which Father and his men would never escape alive.

Those words sent a chill down my spine. The danger Mr. Douglass spoke of was real indeed. Yet Father refused to heed the warning. His mind was fixed on the thousands of guns stored in the arsenal. He needed those weapons to arm the slaves and spread the revolt throughout the South.

Father traveled south to prepare for the attack. Soon after he left he wrote that he had rented a farmhouse in Maryland, five miles north of Harpers Ferry.

Nestled among mountains where the Potomac and Shenandoah rivers meet, Harpers Ferry was, in Father's opinion, far from a trap. Rather, he said, the mountains of the Blue Ridge offered natural fortification that would conceal the activities of his liberation army. Meanwhile, escaped slaves only had to wade across shallow places in the Potomac.

As the weeks passed he often wrote about the volunteers who came to help him fight. Some were ex-slaves, others were white soldiers, and a few even came from Canada.

My brothers Owen and Oliver went with Father. When I learned that another brother, Watson, was planning to join them, I was determined to leave with him. I knew I could make a difference by being there.

As if he had read my mind, Father wrote Mother to ask if she and I would come and live in the farmhouse for a short time. He was afraid the neighbors were suspicious of the unusual group of men living under one roof. Having women around would make it look more like a family farm.

Mother didn't want to leave my younger sister in New York, but she allowed me to go with my sister-in-law, cautioning me, "Annie, please be careful. You may be sixteen years old, but you are not a soldier, young lady. Listen to your father and Martha. Stay out of danger."

It was mid-July when Martha and I arrived. Father's letters had described how cramped the living space was—how true! Eventually more than twenty men lived in the two-story house.

Martha cooked and did the laundry, while I kept constant watch for snooping neighbors. Sometimes I would sit on the porch of the house or stand at the windows so they would see me and think everything was normal.

Little did the neighbors know, our farmhouse held all the weapons needed for a small war! There were two hundred rifles, an equal number of pistols, and one thousand pikes.

At the end of September the time for the raid drew near. Father sent Martha and me back to North Elba.

The morning we left I hugged him for a long time because I could already imagine the dangers he would face.

He told me not to worry, saying he planned to carry a famous sword into his battle. He would capture it from the great-grandnephew of George Washington, Colonel Lewis W. Washington, who lived nearby. Father believed that President Washington's sword would empower him to led this new fight for freedom.

The fateful night of Sunday, October 16, 1859, Father and eighteen of his men marched into Harpers Ferry. They succeeded in seizing the arsenal and several buildings without firing a single shot. By morning the townspeople discovered the raiders and began to fight back. Then a company of marines led by Lieutenant Colonel Robert E. Lee arrived to reinforce the local troops.

The fighting lasted almost two days. When it was over Father was wounded and four townspeople and ten of Father's men were dead—including my brothers Oliver (Martha's husband) and Watson. Newspapers across the country reported every detail of the trial, which was held during the last two weeks of October in Charles Town, Virginia. On October 31, the jury took only forty-five minutes to reach its decision. They found Father guilty of treason against the Commonwealth of Virginia, conspiring with slaves to rebel, and murder.

On December 1, my mother visited him in jail where they talked and prayed together for several hours. I wished I could have been there to tell Father how courageous I thought he was.

He was executed the next morning.

Father's raid did not end slavery. But historians said that it was one of the most important events leading to the Civil War, which began in April 1861. The war destroyed slavery forever in our country, but it also took 619,000 lives and ruined millions of dollars worth of property. My Father must have known this would come to pass, for the day he was hanged he wrote: "I, John Brown, am now quite certain that the crimes of this guilty land will never be purged away but with Blood."

Years after Father's death, I still had sleepless nights. Sometimes I recalled our conversations. Other times I found comfort in the verse of a song that Union soldiers sang about Father when they marched into battle.

His sacrifice we share! Our sword will victory crown!
For freedom and the right remember old John Brown!
His soul is marching on.

Yes indeed, I think to myself, one man against slavery did make a difference.

ROBERT Harper never dreamed his village would become the epicenter of slave revolt. One hundred and twelve years before John Brown's 1859 raid, the architect and millwright established his home at the confluence of the Potomac and Shenandoah rivers, where nature's power had carved a lovely water gap through the Blue Ridge. Against this backdrop of beauty that Thomas Jefferson called "stupendous" and "worth a voyage across the Atlantic," cast the shadow of human bondage—Harper was a slaveowner.

John Brown's raid at Harpers Ferry attempted to erase the shadow of slavery. Brown failed, but his efforts sent shockwaves through the nation. One Southern newspaper claimed that Brown's raid did more to advance the cause of disunion "than any other event since the formation of the Government." A northern poet countered by christening Brown "a saint" who made the "gallows glorious like the cross." John Brown's action drove a wedge between North and South; after October 16, 1859, there was no middle ground in America's struggle with slavery.

In 1944, eighty-five years after the raid, the United States Congress established a national park at Harpers Ferry to commemorate the historic events that occurred here. Today, more than half a million visitors a year travel to Harpers Ferry to learn about the industrial and transportation revolutions, John Brown's raid, the Civil War, and African-American history. Few places have experienced so much history.

Dennis E. Frye
Chief Historian
Harpers Ferry National Historic Park

Top: John Brown in 1859; center: Harpers Ferry, Virginia, in 1857; bottom: Annie Brown with her mother, Mary Ann Day, and her sister, Sarah, in 1851.

JACOB Lawrence is the most renowned African-American artist living today.

Born in Atlantic City, New Jersey, in 1917, Lawrence's artistic talent was recognized when he was very young. As a teenager he dedicated himself to painting and, although he supported himself in various other ways, he never waivered from this commitment. In 1930, when Lawrence was thirteen and living in New York, his mother enrolled him in after-school art classes at Utopia House. At the same time he attended meetings of a Negro history club at the Harlem YMCA. Lawrence has stated, "It was in a Negro history club and our nearly all black schools that I first heard the stories of Frederick Douglass, Harriet Tubman, Toussaint L'Ouverture, Nat Turner, Denmark Vesey, and John Brown along with many others . . . and these stories were told in a very dramatic way."

At age fifteen, Lawrence studied at the Harlem Art Workshop with a leading black artist, Charles Alston, who was impressed with the ability of this quiet, gifted boy. Alston encouraged him. Lawrence broadened his knowledge of art by reading art books at the workshop and he would walk the sixty or so blocks from his home in Harlem to visit the Metropolitan Museum of Art. He continued his studies, receiving a working scholarship to the American Artists School in 1937, when he was twenty.

In the late 1930s and early 1940s, Lawrence painted four different series based on historic individuals connected with the struggle to abolish slavery: Toussaint L'Ouverture, Frederick Douglass, John Brown, and Harriet Tubman. He also created a sixty-painting series depicting the migration of the Negro from the South to northern cities after World War I.

Lawrence served in the Coast Guard during World War II. After the war he resumed his artistic career and enjoyed continued success. His work has been exhibited in

Jacob Lawrence

leading museums in the United States and Europe, and also in Africa. For the past two decades he has taught at the University of Washington, Seattle, where he is now Professor Emeritus.

From his early historical series such as John Brown to his depictions of contemporary black life, Lawrence has been devoted to the portrayal of the human condition. His work is remarkable for its bold use of color, its striking patterns, and strong design. In the *John Brown* series, religious piety, fanaticism, violence, and tragedy are expressed in powerful, pictorial terms.

The Detroit Institute of Arts was fortunate to receive the complete *John Brown* series of twenty-two gouache paintings as a gift from Mr. and Mrs. Milton Lowenthal in 1955. It is one of the treasures of our permanent collection.

Ellen Sharp
Curator of Graphic Arts
The Detroit Institute of Arts

To my husband, Ralph, for encouraging me, to my son, Jason, for inspiring me, to my mother, Dorothy, for always being there when I need her, and to my aunts, uncles, cousins, and friends for having faith in me.

Special thanks to Kim Harbour, whose vision and expert editing made this possible; and to Ruth Hill, Harry Jackson, Mia Morrison, Mercedes Morrison, Deborah Thomas, and Maria Salvador for reading the manuscript.

Editor's note: Jacob Lawrence executed the *John Brown* series in gouache on paper. The dimensions of his paintings are either 13⅛ x 19¹³⁄₁₆ or 19¹³⁄₁₆ x 13⅛ inches, depending on their format. Sixteen of the series' twenty-two paintings are featured here, making this the first time a sequence of images from the *John Brown* series (accession number DIA 55.354.1-22) has been published in color in a book format. Special thanks goes to the Detroit Institute of Arts, Publications Director Julia Henshaw, Ellen Sharp, and the DIA photography department for making new transparencies that capture the vibrancy of these now fragile paintings.

The selection and sequencing of the paintings were made by the author and Rizzoli with the permission of the DIA and in consultation with the park historians at Harpers Ferry National Historical Park. We wish to thank Dennis Frye, Curator Frank Schultz-Depalo, and David Larsen from the National Park Service for their insights into John Brown and for helping to make this story historically accurate.

We gratefully acknowledge Jacob Lawrence's support of this project.

First published in the United States of America in 1993 by Rizzoli International Publications, Inc.
300 Park Avenue South, New York NY 10010

Text Copyright © 1993 by Gwen Everett
Art Copyright © 1993 by Founders Society The Detroit Institute of Arts

Cataloging-in-Publication Data for this book is available from the Library of Congress

ISBN: 0-8478-1702-4

Designed by José Conde
Edited by Kimberly Harbour

Printed and bound in Singapore

Illustrations from the *John Brown* series by Jacob Lawrence:
Cover: Number 6, *John Brown formed an organization among the colored people of the Adirondack woods to resist the capture of any fugitive slave.*

Page 2: Number 2, *For 40 years, John Brown reflected on the hopeless and miserable condition of the slaves.*

Pages 4–5: Number 17, *John Brown remained a full winter in Canada, drilling Negroes for his coming raid on Harpers Ferry.*

Pages 6–7: Number 9, *Kansas was now the skirmish ground of the Civil War.*

Pages 8–9: Number 11, *John Brown took to guerilla warfare.*

Page 10: Number 12, *John Brown's victory at Black Jack drove those pro-slavery to new fury, and those who were anti-slavery to new efforts.*

Page 11: Number 4, *His adventures failing him, he accepted poverty.*

Pages 12–13: Number 13, *John Brown, after long meditation, planned to fortify himself somewhere in the mountains of Virginia or Tennessee and there make raids on the surrounding plantations, freeing slaves.*

Pages 14–15: Number 7, *To the people he found worthy of his trust, he communicated his plans.*

Page 17: Number 15, *John Brown made many trips to Canada organizing for his assault on Harpers Ferry.*

Page 18: Number 5, *John Brown, while tending his flock in Ohio, first communicated with his sons and daughters his plans of attacking slavery by force.*

Pages 20–21: Number 8, *John Brown's first thought of the place where he would make his attack came to him while surveying land for Oberlin College in West Virginia.*[1]

Page 22: Number 18, *July 3, 1859, John Brown stocked an old barn with guns and ammunitions. He was ready to strike his first blow at slavery.*

Page 24–25: Number 20, *John Brown held Harpers Ferry for 12 hours. His defeat was a few hours off.*[2]

Pages 26–27: Number 19, *Sunday, October 16, 1859, John Brown with a company of 21 men, white and black, marched on Harpers Ferry.*[3]

Page 29 and back cover: Number 21, *After John Brown's capture, he was put on trial for his life in Charles Town, Virginia (now West Virginia).*

Notes:
[1] West Virginia was part of Virginia during this time.
[2] Brown held Harpers Ferry for 36 hours.
[3] The troop that marched on Harpers Ferry was made up of nineteen men, including Brown.